Chantry

Chantry

Elizabeth Treadwell

chax

2004

My thanks to the editors and publishers of the publications in which some of this work first appeared: *canwehaveourballback.com*, *Cauldron & Net*, *Duration*, *Elixir*, *The European-San Francisco Poetry Festival Book* (2001), *Iris Rising: the Goddess in the New Aeon* (anthology, Temple of Isis L.A., 2000), *Ixnay*, the *Ixnay* anthology 2003, *Kenning*, *Lit City Broadsides*, *LUNGFULL!*, *Mirage #4/Period(ical)*, *Moria*, *nocturnes (re)view of the literary arts*, *One Hundred Days* (anthology, Barque Press, 2001), *Outlet*, *Rooms*, *Shampoo*, *So To Speak*, *Syllogism*, and *The World*. "the milk bees" first appeared as the title poem of a pamphlet in the Lucille Series, January 2000.

I am grateful as well to Cydney Chadwick and Susan Smith Nash, for early kindness and enthusiasm; to Arielle Greenberg and Carol Mirakove, for friendships struck in poetry travels; and particularly to Charles Alexander, for his care with this book.

The italic phrases in "Christines I-IX" are taken from *The Writings of Christine de Pizan*, ed. Charity Cannon Willard (Persea Books, 1994). The poem's rhythm is in imitation of Willard's translation of Christine's "The Seven Allegorized Psalms," themselves modeled after the Seven Penitential Psalms in the Old Testament. Christine defined allegory as "the use of Holy Scripture for the edification of the soul residing in this miserable world" (she was not always so gloomy, however).

Supported by the Tucson Pima Arts Council and by the Arizona Commission on the Arts with funding from the State of Arizona and the National Endowment for the Arts.

ISBN 0-925904-40-6

Chax Press / 101 W. Sixth St. / Tucson, Arizona 85701-1000 / USA

for Mom

with love

Contents

CHRISTINES I-IX

after Christine de Pizan

I. Like the vessel without a cover

My dear, your fate will not begin, yet of you many chamber quick, you single
frank unknowing & whence proclaim beloved & grasped at, I gladden next
respect to you, pity I. You city you forsaken (set-piece did acknowledge:
progeny of Rome or Salem, do not sorrow gently if not by each alone next
generation, which you might aggrieve & rescue, many from a diplomatic
journey, for this state of state of state, and also next to, rock star, buyer, not to
mention. And please release & gladden next, treaty of them, author of all
_____, such gladden & membership, the risen archive, & notes project
upon concrete wall. Valentine my prescriptive, by way of egged-on fruit,
whichever place I, & sanctity for you surrender, disarm, banish

II. Like a pelican in the wilderness; like an owl in its habitation

This one, Sir, alters toward progeny & lends its toothpaste to retrieve it, but,
Sir, you are the Real, Sir punished on the narrow, altered unto in mince
archive, in that, Sir (*that is Thy people*) to recover, dear you water with
entrail. My dear dear, request I narrate of them, unmarked & grave, & Sir's
happy & empty formative, that Sir won't quell my sugar I, my bleeding
narrative & my own limbs of desiring next to unkempt envy quote frocks of
hers, hers, march type of figured speech, if not quarrel, desertion, madness,
stolen item. Protect your underling Sir from I beg of Sir

III. These things will be written and ordained for the generations to come: and the people yet unborn shall praise our

Next to shrubbery, yours, your still-life rendezvous is deja'd, certain, add to it
it with certain, so while I sugar Sir can I squarely, because scant conundrum,
for naturally this quiet *with which Thou didst bear* your several arches, in
certain statesmen, in certain times, and of them, acquaintance, proper
recipient, the narrow ancestor, of them nearby, particularly personages of
requesting, of of of a place of which, and remedy, and sugar. Yes unload
them, Sir oh Sir, consider with undoing, with *lighten* with, as I. Next layer to

9

I whither prize in quicken, so in me lead me and them

IV. (or Addenda: Christine de P.'s Sex Writing)

press **Anonymous Composer**, beggar, braggart, enemy. You're not even
[illegal variant of her name]. She disowns or unrelies me, see.
Winterstitch cocktail, peaked swarm. Miserable snowcap. In my **birth life**
I do not behave in that manner.

V. Therefore they declare the name

My you caught certain have then save most near vary, if then by one mirror
of partake which by housing we can grace Sir's placate, hope by Sir, many
greedy for one burgeoned headcap so cruelly poking which lingered variant
Sir, fairchild, *present & to come,* sugar them in taking. Aggregate charm in
corpus of, with nary much of trinkets and of tools to grope to cleanse with,
able portrait altogether remain of course in that with which, certitude,
wealth reside therein, replicating constant goods, earned negligence, when,
by your leave, imprison. When pleased so serve I care of need, when exist
can, for devour merry to sugar Sir

VI. Like a beast without a collar

run shadow run shadow run hollow

(like a maid alert farewell)

VII. In the beginning

Um, Sir definitely every, by Sir with kindness only pictograph recommend
lonely sacrifice by end only narrow, narrow sharklike set their solemn
demarcation by your favorite, by senator, by megastar, merge for Sir — might
I call you Sir — which you might linger forward several naturally and fully,
marking and caressing this pressed to this enemy. Bequeath it next — for I
sugar Sir — might able signature undo these lost

10

VIII. Do not hide Thy face

Situate hole on I, dear Sir, for crest such vista I delay, and now now this plea of Sir I certain moniker hope's benefit native sugar, on hence carried site of today Sir, you manacle of thus, sugared of high then Sir bowed *to be born of a woman in a poor common place among dumb beasts*; hence Sir, sweet charge honey Sir, mannered Sophist, long able in making hour cream, of natural mini-torso then feed upon nearby coldly link. Sir you many over straw pleats thereby, will this sugar Sir, oh my kitten your Dear Truncated of highest trinket and piece held up esteem forebear quite. Can we ever make up to greed, for lingering or sweeten one incorrectly no quite; can we please unsugar see that Sir, you may fetch of utter cream. Forget I not, Sir, when my circumstance

IX. shalt endure

Over Sir you Many very purpose you are over high situation watchful many because my asking narrow of remember in each sugar sent over Sir from Sir's faithful Sir, corny obtuse, link yet landscape via hors d'oeuvre prior kid's upset, sugaring Sir only kid narrow has to unsweet glassware, that horrid ending thence in linkage so upset bodily so sweaty then last hellbent river outside our courtyard will this sugar of rename that I won't compensate unduly in the orchid hell of that one which shuddered bodily might narrow I for cleaning bits. Yet linger so this grace of grace we can clear this item of gradation to our kin and narrow sugar so we can do for such ever bits as want as do.

half-life.

it gives little embellished betterment, self-service somehow in the relation cupboard hilarity coup. frontiersville's mega-bell. the gnawing teeth of synthetic velvet clauses. smells like earl grey tea. *(Vanessa io)* fig. concave interruption of outline. circularly inward upon herself. against walls of emanation. corona fondling happens along, unique in this sense: "facing away". little more than an urban industrial swamp, shimmering pickleweed, seen a dozen party boats. presented affiliation programme, make eye contact. when meeting a child in the tide-nurtured marshes. restoration browse, legally in late summer, torn down the probability anatomy sparks. complex in the course of a corresponding ebb. the branches spun twig courtship unhurriedly. intertwine some private postcoital room. streams of grasses; thick molten shadows seen in public species. debris hibernates offices admittedly pressures rolled into one. Vanessa! all the heads had approximately the same surgeries. jerks his leg away, a setback. because it occurs to her to protrude from this setback. cultivated space, sensory point hatching fluctuating mothers of more specific input dissolves the passion input, we are shining. colonies of flowers. tiny hammers. violets. roses. carnations. calla lilies. globe thistle. limes. equipped to rival the roseate semidarkness. decorous, undiminished constellations. potential sexual partners orienting stimuli, trying in advance, Vanessa! keep discreet watch over their nuptials. sweet-smelling accessibility, stubborn forehead. syndrome application snapped up. a great inland "reclamation", the last last regurgitory refuge. self-guided facilities, the glinting approach of any creature to rot. flowers, roped off on a balcony, the way out at dawn.

is then given and eaten at once. no test. narrower kilter, one's tongue.

Fidelity

everyone has known
this age of our lord in his death throes, tattooed seams
down her legs in the cafe, the saving of bits of
bush, lamplit wondermount

surrounding the children are animal figurines and
his son, portraits of muleback visitors, the boulder wedged
in a slotback canyon, fingers crook working with chocolate
tuiles and mousse, couple found a locale that felt like

people probably realize that this is a place I'd always
dreamed of, actually a network adaptation to the future,
Mary along a road, an array of old milk cartons standing in rows
for a quarter mile protected new trees

prepared to cave in, still to stop salty groundwater, including
information really there to tell us, in other words, what we
should have know from oblivion, the difference between
thickheadedness and a smile

which is only six million years old, youthfully urbane, a geologic
ghost, abandoned by its crew, very delicate wide-open spaces,
grace of ultra, its slope littered with blocks cut from nearby cliffs
and hauled here long ago, probably smaller

museum case, rebuild the province, scoff led by was apparent,
legendary, we must thank him for this, but we
have no interest, natural homes, weapons that may have belonged
to laughter, orphans take a ride

I do this, I have needed him, males filled with tension, represent
plaintively, appeared, dance beneath simply platinum
tones, horses needed to certify the plenitude, if the second hungry
purse

fresco transferred to canvas, mounted to panel, measure usually
happens out there, synchronized chaos from innovation to results,
claimed a lead to underemployed believed to repulse dialectical
past rid, conducted cleansing, their own country, don't they?

composition

waitress of mercy glance in the hollow tube underwear glen. dear calamity profile, hunky bearer of wand and limbs. Newton's alchemical harpooned state dreams like argyle roughage. she was a literalist in the tradition of wander mer. time being nonsense water, vapid arcane hands translate the ice floes though had jumped bikini wooden. eyes catch alert old lantern motion in the nightmare pretty prevalence from the camera to the bone, in the acid prep vein, the foreskin pursuit of tilted twisty. there's a right time to be inverted, ripe with fever drowning amid. more closely loosely goodybelt. ten clouds nudes softly mutiny softly crazy dollhouse pale attic floor. a fine fabric of darkly pressed silk. opinion in steel terms of distance. on the individual not the person fashion inspired by staircase dreams. the dark and unclothed streets even unlatch measures, flesh, vocabulary, cootie, amazingly, church and stereos. perceive grainy houses, cousin. polyfield fidelity. the constant bulletin borne of already modern sunshine. don't debt perceive her shoulders, her sharp quick pimple dildo like punctuation.

The City (Plastica)

tours are given in English every day, most high and honored lady,
though both are as white as somebody off The Brady Bunch,
I'm sick, sophisticated women, who also invented wood trim,
the sidewalk irreverent, remained close to her friend from the pre-war days,
hairpin turn and after this gas balloon pretending to be
a residence, produced mindspray, prudence, whirligig, night and day she prayed
for pregnant women, the task come into port—

turned to stone, because his enemies live at a youth camp in the mountains,
climb over the fence and redefine that messenger of love,
ungirdled in pavillion performances, considered no formal
education, brought heed to the ghost, so locked it in place,
discussion following victories, translation, innate generosity—

they walked, trying to wake up while checking out all the weird folk,
marriage of their daughters will force them to pay, though
knucklehead standing in the roof, floorboard, cabinet,
a large chair—
singular dissolves, staring, extraordinarily, from the porch,
pays witness, cordless, gladly see that she don't need the fig image,
reciprocity but only with themselves

sexual merely long drives, commotion is going on, votive
present, bowls painted— little evening with a bedroom stove,
mouth abolishes original being, to plow the earth inhabit a great boon fountain,
not propaganda, customers, fleece at this address,
I believe that you resemble walk five surrounded by a crimson first—

category mended promise and hopelessness, new stocking
to see which of his relatives is recast, here again, never the sooner, hung
around noble themselves dispatched, grabbed the handle steps,
but time implies a voice first, and a tennis court, heading back
will continue to fail golden vice, warm entreaty, standard courtesy,
continue down, the artists moved stunned, funny, too late

fleur de lys

complect anime & the horse stop,
a girl musician tells all in the airport lounge — o o
her uncle, her type of rice, her children —
lantana signature, ici! don't be too scared, the false
title flower, alligator baby, our lady of easy
destined — it is known or has been known
by people, properly ovation denying she
is the root, bulby yellowpinks on the runway,
you can tell me one thing, & i'll tell you
another. pudding evenings, Euterpe's daylilies
among all my daughters, that's just too much
city for me, duckweed, palmetto, the females
make the choice, just like with humans —
spanish moss filled mattresses, wingback
victoriana, cottonmouth. took the streetcar
harsh tagged trashcan, even the air
is more ornate, flowers that look like vases,
the cotton exchange, the aboveground
cemetery one time dwelling, beveled dove,
our lady of prompt, then there's like
this freeway, no, i haven't formed any
concrete opinion yet, two diamond grapefruit,
old soprano photo, Barbie, Darcie, Ashley,
Shawn. pick apart Lenten compromise,
you bumpy, driven muses — our native
mother whatsay — o, cypress
knees, crepe myrtle, city of creamy
disease & orchestration —

Tigerpups

elephants in embroidered skullcaps — men with skinny arms dancing — length of birdtail — silhouetted tree — tigers, tiger pups, the man who claims them — blue television halflight skimming — our naked, North American, bodies — blind hum of sheet and scarf —

Tenderly Particles of Steel

manifest letter revived in memorial bucking lot, not so now, crinoline frames anybody who standing in the sun police foreground made up golden lanterns, mother's garage, should things held grave, with asleep room loitered, another looking at the sky with rubbed breath-mist, sandy gossip, chortle little narrow definite, so we can have history, metaphor, bas-relief, bloodthirsty banisters half-century elliptical amendation, too close can't hear

that mud moths, silver, mottled and scarlet money, tools of eyebrow passivity, piss and shit ontology, attached offering find a candy riddle, be had which had, which had pandora echo, screen information groups of consequent earmark, the sacred intelligent animal, paranormal, its art and there, day of closure, transformed concept, live without our terror letters, instant portal "good morning" occasionally nearer lady m., bought decorative

holding to them, all jointly countrymap, speaking to any picture, but again, they said fair bad stuff, bathed and consummated, deployed the copied shape, in a field is a circle of battered eaten, grass in the sun and she falls asleep there, stolen counted, potent immodest denim methodology, bric-a-brac coding ties hygiene interval, few fruits embellish by jumping, myths catch up to my nervousness, everyone should recurring

a ravenous tempernance, skew thankless underfur, gray morning was a nothingness, new birds, new places, babe in quantify tempted, a clock stuck, little governess taken a smile on library, peddling stuff into her eyes, everyday nightclubs women are into a thin line, clasped gloves, a lot of dresses cheap ok, powder all over my shoulder, struggling in the window, the mind as well as the body, but please, across the hall having her hair washed

for Janet Frame

notoriety

europa came into port, always ridin'. vague shut-up towards freedom, on the bench laced warmest attractive essential. chauffeur flinging to her feet. america burst into the room off that radio fiend, the saturday paper molten cocktail a little sadly. hair combed straight, flocks of caviar horseshoe. yo about, her calling up lieutenant wine and sipping proper apartment flurry. enchanting sidecar in the middle of bed. the man acquired what a drag opportunity with light hair everything acolytes. demanded in a stage drink, her rogue stick murmur, money lynx. plenty burning sleepin' right, glad.

been goldy star during joke dumpy toppling space-black nation. smash toward the address. hot furiously pressed her cheek against his. get away from anything, the admirin' summoning ridge dancin' wide awake, your crackly legs. girl in the name of all that's holdin' you back. extremely shave the following presence. we did it back home.

this minute red sofa coldly handsome dame parade our lust the bearcat got the dope. 'cept wad of sailing folks publicity, preserve-closet, prominent like a sheath of madness with primitive champ caresses, feeling the lining, the half-pint with regret.

astonishment whiskey two flats to each floor, lordly sepulchre. there was no one trying to pacify her. crepe sweat in spite of all the piled diamond plenty. to drive the avalanche terpsichore afternoon forcing upward. expectin' hosiery fueled plenty narrowly. subscription told about. overhead plume snake regards us fruitless senior punching. rub scrap heap feebly intimate strips of cloth for her need. gamble dull and continuous ink upon bright pans. limbs training dollar moments vestige a lady here, eyes dropped from her and looked again.

Torn/town

Troy Silver

I I have been constant any future tragedies he he died for the sea
rose-water redhead. Blacken as anterior baldric Alexandria allegiance.
Remove from a particular place. Align. The excess of multistage
refinery. Her Ingrid will wear inclement. Tokyo color girls hidden
in leafy portfolio he he bought me. A bottled glass made to L.B. LAB,
INC. Hollywood California. Cuts or sets vessel. Clementine serpentine
but this is not a history! Paperclipped, susceptible canard. Dislocate
regionality survey. Inches of cities. Quadruple.

Venda Johnson was lovely to look at. She picked up.

In silver silver Troy. Wrongful concealment mispronounced. This lends
you. Hebe: cupbearer of the gods before. Hard, brittle, grayish white.
Promoting embargo harpoon accustom. Neurology free from combination.
Her sister was privy civilian. Hebe: cast off. Of frozen jailer.
Ingrid Stone antebellum glint. Eternal chauffeur. Pussy-cup.
Braggadocio congest. Humane pimp, crinoline. Associate entry hooked
by ex cathedra. Douche. Re-embark tissue structure lowlife.
Disjointed bowline. Apple cake. Eden: Adam. xx: Adonis. Hebe:
sylphlike cross stone dolly. Enclosed garden: host, ladyluck. Pig!
Spiral Japan: postcard ice cream both single and Mesopotamian. Where
is

rounded and supported it. 'during the cosmic night she will give birth
to a daughter sun', 'she appears...dotted &'

Interchangeable logos present compounding minuet. Artemis of unknown.
Her tangled diary
                                    becomes punk-rock hoes flattened land
in film fields painting the

                                    quite still oxygen. 'That she
should be the mother of the forerunner was revealed'

Most ancient Tonio. Troy, whatever else may be, oh adrenaline.

Porcelain inky. New elocution. Antisocial pastern, Queen of the May

caw caw caw prosody

importune patristic clemency — bum bag. bitchily reach rolling pin
rolling drunk junk mill.   Careless duel framed above board.
The relationship of these two, photograph and painting. Babysit
accessory with an indirect maneuver. Before elusive north north west.
Ado heal. Discountenance. Supernatural erections, oracles. Perversion
of fostering, since by rejecting habit rely. Prepare fashion funk
propertied. Feast, heckle and school

He he died by the river. Torn/town

no immediate compromise

ex cathedra parasol. unabated. I should never have told her anything
(to follow Troy Silver).

He he died sued for the sea.

                baby cyclops murder

(another Western) alibi. 'I kept moving my free hand over her warm
body.' Cattle hook cross saltire: she was something else. Lives in
broken down: we are at the stone half wall. John trickling daffodil.
Babies buried in this land, eons. Fairy circle:

                                      cross to headstone memorize. Laguna. Flynn's.
Trees include this bubbled ground & oxen led away. Oh Laura; these
treatises quick and slow on the way to the gangway—

'stayed home on holidays; she did the same' a kindness metabolize
queasy reef rollerblind metamorphose.

Electronvolt frontier confection. Everyday whip, reestablish, thrall.

In semidetached contusion mangle. Quit tirade tire— underpaid massacre.
In gulls land. Very few. Hob nob edition carryall. Logic swamp
giveaway. Buck and seal. Janey provision brandy-snap. The way west,
Edith: 'he hardly knew what prompted him to utter the wish, poor thing'.
It might not scathingly.

Because the Cherokee did not cry. Library she was since I had collapsed
the crudest way. I'll agree slipped into. Oval supine. Precognition
when dark nursling precut party favor. Underhanded for this new wound.
Kingcup racket. Relinquishing expedition. Well-earned purulent
resemblance. Ownership of an unoccupied fourfold. Born to sing her
song of shame.

Parochial begonia talkative wax. Oh Troy, parlour game. Undermentioned
shanty; splintery galantine and valentine. Her fingers softly dangle
there. Stoop undreamed full-term. Qualify rummy epic. No no metronome

moll rush tenant farmer. (1840, price one penny)

Looker-on sea tract. The mass of school-age refractory. Neutralize,
copulate epoch. Minibus informant quit because ninefold, Christianized.
Nonliving coterie. Count one, a person, anybody. Breed

the state of overlapping propeller

                                   gloss crow brethren full of glory
stricture   oh inebriate animalia

sustain   twist   vegetate   pine

Handful

Immobilize life force lecture. As your features see right through
you. Lie bottom purse. Remnant of conscience wherein lurked. '—
breasts so large that they're interesting only as freaks of nature'
Saigon playground witches. Inside Cadillac kaleidoscope egret. Daisy
or pearl. Constant mirror. Trial of minor maryjane footstepped.
He may have ended with nothing. Under shotput tree. Kind waitress.

Swearword masseur. And during the past week I'd. Ordinary temperatures
team on the field. And because pause. Nondata. The heart is commonly.
Monster. What was she thinking.

Be happy that you can keep remove strangeness housebroken. Being
characterized by rich diversity. Single friendship. Houseboat our
indicators she drove a silver wedge spike heel fraternity. Languishing

        space a brief potted passion. Foresister hysterectomy.
Snot boy prudishly. Rumpus. Insemination in artificial wonder. Gaunt
conductor. Unguent. Suburban cladding. Pocket: a report of speech.
Large predatory unparalleled elegant.

While they shift blame, remain psychiatrically.

Often contemporary. Within declared competent. Highlights the fact
that I know I am asking you a trifle mantelpiece so flagrant. Tea.
'You take her from me at a stroke I suppose.' Moment for Jack. Yuan
sat up in bed. Agnes Mary. Flying cloud first born obedient. A short
cognate in the elementary world.

The child child child. And others hurt deeply. He was a genius,
skinned alive.

        three pennies to the altarpiece. Bubbleland
sedated. Failure of the house.

        subjunctive crustacean.
In the deep deep summer lighthead fancy. Dymphna

He he thought of marriage. The other alchemy. Sit down. Troy Silver.

Indecipher. Not even tasting. Economic historically absent. Blood
— a grandson; no explanation. Steal his mannered style. Wealthy,
large, square. Vertigo celebrated. Quirky instant modify. Bruised
young ripe. Name your character, Olive:

                                                    the discovery that
spoiled

rich in landing

                                                        Rhetorical temptress
panoramic aggregation baptize. Altruism postulate. Captain filthy
repudiate. Pure dilation average. Apparently lectern grubby assurance.
Disentangle adoption flotilla infidel. Cynosure damnable. Substantial
almanac repatriate term.

Strike comfort appeal. In the dark bar furrow gab triple trice wore
integrate. Canker agnostic lovely pretended. Avid upshot undermine
dilapidation. Great terrible entertain fluttering family.

Banal anthem exponent moving or directed toward the sky's beau monde
introduction. Equal cheat. Source turning accusation. How to all
this if. Restive teamster. Troubleshoot. A mythical vortex. Legacy
forward sweltering average.

Rocket sort. Quaint spectrum wilt holding rank. Bounce trivial winter.
I screamed out, Charles. Unify, demean. Preface damage examinate.
Technical vow conditional.

livestock. Ancient stenography. Take kindly stratify unfaithful weary
sustenance. Couples' attempts reported 'very weak'. Fifties song
unpainted.

Decade tendency yield. Patricia as they. Generic metacarpal.

Tunnel rose ambassador. Along oil on canvas. Grapnel farmyard.
Sphere's center cavern. Floating bespectacled. Amber orifice. Feature
of sozzled overfond. Adapt medallion stride. Megavolt immunity.
Regularly buff. Make use of desirable catastrophe breath.

Intersect plump tribe. Subordinate particular crossroad. Lily:
franchise upper torch. Reeds ordained and precious handbag.

Skulls granted Jupiter as seen on lessons. The name of subject through
space bound. Star of the usually citizen. Six branches traditional
alcohol. Troublesome New York Friday. Cloister passing by extension.
Imagine toiling relic. Dropped from the forgotten divination. Double

26

diamond bone. 'angels in a nuptial chamber...Sophia & the Redeemer.'

Veil lifegiving scarless imp. Empire brightest numbers to place a
nail. Baldric valentine. Razors fictitious fleeing arena. Her head
neither backfire. Sections imported whatsoever Jesus. The later,
classical, perpetual charms after all.

Amorphous maiden but not their trump shedding mock. Only theory
falcons. Mascot atomic touchstone. Unnamed misfortune who generally.
Slain favor bears no. Properly born causing infinity crocodile.
Chariot republic yet no one carved. Associated exceptional kings and
fourwheel diction. Custom copied from his/her

unpronounceable location

Leisurely Pile-up

Delicate next door. Anjali impose. After four years as a corporate
I'll never forget.

Liberties in cross wing. Self-indulgent ewe. Sandblock arcade. Repeal
me in an unknown state.

Happen leave. There is a sound. Most accurate miniskirt. Torture
halfway.

Storm door cogitate. Of cyclone bourgeoisie. Contest trial. Secure
interruption were not as. Near their half-bald care party to an origin.
Oh precarious nation. Outstanding

corpulent. Corollary predestination. Register heresy — to make a
stolid flowery. Gunpowder middleman. Basket spur rhapsodic desolate.
Basilica stalking-horse. Please no more! Jejune persistent assuredly.

Sedan odalisque. Her stem and dispersion. Provocation clap-trap.
It pains inhale. How doves do hamstring gossamer recording. Infer
cyclotron. Move indignant eerie. A formal outrage. Mix-up; inflame.
Address extrasensory. Coexist social work pixie. Gratuitous
benefactor.

Killjoy notional. Bowdlerize dusk. Overhead manservant. Nothing
dowager. Suspend pale jingo. Nicety layer jimmy contention. Medieval
flirtation clank. Crouch spike irritate. Julian of Norwich.
Suspenders. Clannish periwinkle.

At hand down the delicate ordeal. Purple compunction integer.
Homograph cuisine. Extraterrestrial gogo. Sweetish protein drift.
Cymbal fearful calculus. Machine shroud mutilate. Wrong feat.
Undercover mouthpiece. Peony sheikdom. Collect a vivid glowing flame.

Done already varnish random. Fringe remark sideboard reveal. Canto
basin evening star. Stupefy clarinet hyperactive. Strident bystander
suspension acre. Compartment gunrunning uniform. Bypass major league.
Keep cement medical. So far as first appears. Sheer offspring

impression. Sham depot. On the basketwork hire. Spank collar moat. Grassland cellblock. Gush electro-mute. Queer bylaw. Spotty thankful masonry. Byzantine controversy. Question cellular blasphemy. Marian algae bribe. Louisiana spigot has done. Rotunda fluff.

Flippant pep talk harpy primarily soot. Standard maze.

Oh Stelline vanguard crystallize. Skew the macabre percale.

in pantomime chanteuse

She wore Hawaiian flowers and a mint-green tread. Tennis visor; cane.
C & H factory rides shoreline. Slipper gold. Remarks & dedication:
transept.

Transsexualize. Agent of. Begot venom (verbiage) discard lozenge
practicum. In Troy, Troy. Thunderously.

Not imminent miscarried. Randall Jones.

Indies our ginger (in Troy, Troy). Baldric seam.

A desert landscape eagle eye. (Influenced by you of course.) Offset
sincerely scrape. Very speculum chrome. Leisurely transestimate.
Manly coattail hobo. She's wearing pants!

Rudy was the looker. I thought all. Estrangement relived.

Body file. Please avenue
                    rub thicker rye.

Object. Nomenclature of her should. Pausing grimly human glee. Why
Jenny gazing not care enough. (1880 middleage)

Decisive sacrifice mandate. Amuse considerable moral, physical
astonishment. For purposes of railroad. Kindly grocery bills. Enough
to keep him. But my spent laurel customary. Estate halcyon of anymore.
The music ceased. He choked without using the word.

Wretched grace. Felt each true conjure. Relish senile agitator.
Embed via ostensible. Automatic pedigree. Discharge brash apoplexy
impulse. Radiant canteen annexation. Mother below protest. Persistent
state of causation. Clay pots therefore needles stand. Upright thorned
in order. Reborn aegis. Interior frolic. Absent observatory
limelight.

Leaves. Echoes of not touching.

objection

Notorious hair. In small, peculiar circumstance. He he died. Caucus lamentable trickle. Philology limpid. Rock bottom hostility. Integer. Tortoise citation. Fourposter compare suck. Gratuity transient temple. Overhaul disjoint backbone.

                         Petroleum carving. Marianne. Midnight divalent. Motherly beverage. Chicory aquarium. Lucinda paralysis. Rocket medical cuisine. Remarkable horizontal. Game plan highboy. Prima donna orthopedics. Interstellar declivity.

Jaunty, bootless.

Correlate unfamiliar macadam. Purport, unload choral decade. Reword indecorum. Governess mason fastening. People dilapidated. Narcotic combination. Galvanism. Etching fact. Installment grandeur. Famous loss. Rudiment. The plastic tower unabridged. Garnet razor.

Adele and Linda. Triplicate manifesto. 'Their father's side'. Orient. Cork black letter. A fairy could transform. Between the wars, diary and journal. Her floating feet. Belated universe. Swaybacked double agent.

          Adele says, balance of upstairs denouement criterion. The tone of Henry. Dungeon Cassandra physical. Neon marigold.

                                    Deerskin and human skin. Spear.

From clear viewing axis. Shaggy pimple carnal arriving. Linda occasionally. Scrubwoman. Scrub.

Days of grace. Chirping in black and white treaty. ...given as follows: n. chief Egyptian god of the underworld, brother and husband of Isis and father of Horus

Glisten outstanding destitute verge. Blemish puppet. Star City is shaken. Cashmere unanimous supplement.

The Proclivity of Isis

Incantation. All reflection.
Super-imbibe. Roustabout
seraphim.

Series of serial. Import acute
birch trumpet. Landed
lady of cardtable. Ceremony
trawl.

        Inside upper treachery.
Unstudied neglect. Delinquent
republic.
        And stunk overtime.

Bullish amalgam. Restore

        Harsh lodging. Na-
vigate residence.

        Redolent injury
tittered & tether

Angelique's Reprisal

1542. A higher higher mention. Ladybug, peeper. Cylinder boredom
bent philosophical. Panic durable. Spotted proper noun. Chime onward
stagecoach packing desperate proposal. In silver, silver. Sheepskin
canticle. Overmix procurer. Second person conservatory. Restorative
standard apropos. Slack preface. Myrmidon.

Unflappable besmirch.

                    Spiders in the yard. Gossip demure. Death
sentence. (Penalty in foreplay.) Ingredient soap opera. Janey
Robbins led astray. Grass widow slyly sharecropper. OK City.

We led her. She produced us. Mixed-up congress records. Listen
shortly. Look. Lively mention.

America the promise. Chocolate supermodel pillow. Over tricorn punk
sorority. Point-blank otherworldly. Percussion ethnology. A meager
tube underfoot. Would-be mutual osmosis. Irrelevant or simply.
Scene ungodly congruent sensationalism. Yonder Yorkshire. Cap inquire
tedious saloon. Telecast denotation. Dakota trilateral profile.
Sopping voidable. Staccato medicine. Unfrock stratum. Unfriendly
honky-tonk.

                    She she sophisticate river. Lacing the fish. Obstinate
half-moon. Lamplit impartial. The first three finishers. Backhand
scarlet fever picturesque. Shapeless history meal ticket. Frolic
and pledge. Modern island distinguished crowd roughly. Hussy.
Puncture resistance. Devotee of iambic flat. Assemblage of
centerpiece. Honorary party line. A rehearsal dinner. In front
of so as to prevent. Instant pueblo. A layer or strip.

Aching guide. Preachy superfluous. Parquet lament. A bird too young.
Pendulum grand slam. Roadside show.

                    Cheyenne hotel resound gold
leaf. Hawaiian echelon. Lydia's husband. Quicken the cusp.
Conductivity in pale gray color. Per capita, lame duck. A chewy

voracious blasphemy. Art deco dining; indigenous rumble seat. Plum blue accolade.

Represent hippodrome.

Scapegrace midland incognito hire. Spot turning binder. This sultry trail.

in clay portrait memorize

figurine that hotel

beauty's narrows; necklaces white shelves; her finery & bottles. she
represents.
really quite unguardedly; today my dirty intersect — white & plastic
squishy — tenderly empty wooden before. The almost-child. Like a
little dead bird on the tile

                                               tearing took the winter — half plastic.

in Florence, she saw a show, the imprint; of men's; of women's;
represent
                        naked by that cross/at the clinic

sectional encounter. Joan, Melina, penny Magdalens. Frank driving.
        coerce discretion; coffee cup; removal

the themes & topics were typically light & satirical   his natural
son; aesthetic: a dancer, acrobat, and mime
                                      for many practical
originated; signed by runes, and so on. Timothy each; condensed city
odes.   Path sought: linely   loss, heretic, bore. abbey
external episodes remaindered   hymn as a pool of   chosen loss
        'In Communion the event is happening now, and it is entirely true.'

(*Teresa of Avila*)

mental transitive   1907: no child stars/six petitions correspond

                   :"Oh, no" she asked

       'I gather that he is impressed but jealous.'   (*Jean Rhys*)

certain places and periods; originally a paradox; there were two main
kinds/ in fact, such movements; this phrase summarizes/ thereby

so-called q.v. 'angry young man'   'There were no movies flickering
like thoughts against a white wall.'   (*E.M. Forster*)

a district famed   A few disciples —1209

his place of penance   skein

acrostic northerner molasses: long-term twinkle
        disconsolate chrysanthemum

                                inhospitable evergreen stamped
personal dystopia

                    she proxy odds & ends   picture clasp
beneath overdrawn glory   appearances in cypress   the same sum

on feast days enrolled   conservation asteroid

he he died by the river   she lingered about it   fairy trees
and recourse   In Troy, Troy   Fallacious nexus!   She screamed

skyscraper: she crossed over the river to the desert, and the story
ends there. Rapid stride, free and clear

                        They go to Paris, learn
bindery   cellular figures of speech

restless, assured restoration.   game and censure: who?   under
the fingernails of the tourist trade, what, how was it made, why?

she longed to imagine perfectly these scenes; she was writing

        one homage and then another; one hotel; colored lights,
advertisement

        beginning with the 5th c., remained most mascot

                                fighting and
lovemaking happened here; promenade; intuition

replace

                                        gregarious cessation

carousel & dinosaur; booty; lingered   so she lingered, gunny sack
and sheen of gown   she had grown very very old   there
was a young one beside who stroked her palm   very quietly

                                        pitch: chloroform

(anesthetic & solvent)

                                        (v.t. daughter-in-law)

distomap for the coded mountains, pale frontier, or
the devotions

for my sisters, Margaret & Carol

"This faith was expressed using symbols of shaped metal, embroidered cloth, carved wood, and painted canvas." —curator, San Xavier Mission, Tucson, Arizona, U.S.A.

in a well-sought dream remember think of something plain like Grammy's tears; think of something plain like the color and curvature of gingerale nightgown & bend & kink of patio, how the 3rd vowel of her name was scratched in.

think of some plain dream of something like how the buildings of a
particular high school became part of your body — its grubby lockers, the
glass of its metal panes, the terrors of gum on things, or, if in Arizona, its
trellised breezeways &

saint-abrasive walls

that one boy's back of head withdrawal crinkly toward your new sugar paws,
the inept hairstyle of a still-favorite teacher (chem lab particular: insulting
miracles, too; with atoms slamming you into that seat all worn out—

why am I a girl

(I'veneverbeenthisfuckedup). in a well-sought dream remember pop song proclamations, Nicole's big shoes and how she tipped them, flirty, Clementine, third grade flat rug, your leotard itch — committing with mastodon eyes the masturbations of Marilyn Monroe — or, mass-produce doodles of *perfect ballerinas*

the decoration of the senses
the pornographic mailbox
widow to the investigation

go home & eat bowls of cereal. the kitchen circa 1903 w/new cabinets

committing with resolute arms
the acts of Cleopatra

lies & other orthographies: my *.

"The water's edge so overgrown with grapes that the surging waves flowed over them —"
— Captain Amadas

The generations changed too quickly & the children began to turn out all weird & bitter.

well sought remember were days and nights of highway the trucker STOP the LOGOS merging with your SIGHT & fear & thrill the Marlboro Menthols with green packaging the digital tune the particular cap the safety the way the truckers stopped and slept the road became quite thin and empty the final Tulsa sunrise sleep in a hospital lot and next, the youngest her warmest warmest coats how she looked up

then also a blue mountain the way its sweatshirt ponytails paraded about the smooth bent of Honda the Honda was our age nearly the sweatshirt was the color of skin or sky or blue mountain so named the photo was full of light our sunglasses formed the darkest spots there were birds there and certain trees, Mom *text itself beats winged*   you tried out—"boiled peanuts & the southern-accented Cherokee waitress"— learning to see past the Bible and Vegas and how it was ALL OK talking past canyons and rivers and shops in the middle of blind flat states called Uncle Junk and how you didn't stop there but stopped there and there was a well-earned you felt dip in a mastodon chlorine—that means you laid down some cash for the Holiday Inn in Rapid City—and in OK City you shared a parking lot teeming with participants in the Red Earth Festival it was July and the guy at the counter gave you a discount thus porch strung about doors stung with conversation you merely listening and near Graceland a nice old German-descended lady said, here take some cookies, GIRLS
cable and frybread and what Grammy remembered and was willing to *give up* or with which to *gamble*

> * *Pocahontas,* your false house & impossible letter,
> crown, marriage, shields, swearing, bending, robe,
> my play on play on play, Rebecca, ornamental
> *bearing —*

codes of the very femininity

a novelette

part i

"We cannot help our Inclinations, Sir"
　　　—Aphra Behn, 'The Luckey Chance'

strut

in the evening it was décolleté, encase themselves, be the dominant. winds do gently, perhaps this supposed rolled in intractable lamp, a Byronic if not diabolic villain, with sticks & stones. "Um, they want to show us off as a new discovery." suspected she knew, down along the pine and crowns. sable arbor on the threshold, but that rich fool must die or none deserve.

husbands & wives

once upon a time what are the conditions that you did tear. for if he may be my friend working outside the home and therefore when I regained your thrones above. much different in relation to, of breeze and leaf are borne their marriage and from marrying. precepts wise, hoarsely, letting you her today, nothing more to me pained.

split open, unable to speak, in exile, a fulness of growth, the present stage, a generous, tattered, humble, so truly pronounced colonies as he died to make men holy for idiots, like thee and I.

holds a part, chariot right, heavens displayed, the burning bush, it under your skin, wind, heteroblur in my throes, subgallant flection on a sudden. hairdressers, the pages in the oscillant men as well.

no longer is the husband able to exercise power as nurse-and-doctor type, much different to his faithful fox. stood by his dilemma. that will cost him to go outside too and to see if the bird faltering she told him hard face to show, rusty and half bright, the maiden from the cupboard began chatting and primarily about the problems of their children's behavior.

to her own devices, sensually beautiful, languorous, to the partner who has
that when a lamb escaped the flock, sprite from life to form to lip. oldest
made fun of reassurance, quickly jumped into bed, which are compassionate.
a mirror whose enhancing comparative availability with high-status husbands,
thence if I follow (hence not mistaken Fame), the difference between
economic depressed. his knees before the sorcerer and all. I was never more
than a girl he was friendly with. he was covered shape would have been more
effective if form so divine.

a reason for marriage

to my decree the kingdom but did not possess the inner resources. with snow
maiden saw the young chevalicr as he came marching. told her flatly assault-
ing noses, work than there would be in many parts. a head where wisdom
mysteries did frame between the dull, law-abiding appalled silence, "my
father's a dying man", but he's on his own feet again. engaged he had had a
very delicate maiden everything I demanded jump to her death. that were
missing the chore, resonant with folklore and song. happened, but I didn't
find him in her present fragile state of mind. whereas now, bath crystals, one
day feathers. the more you love romance...the more you'll love this offer.

after them about to dive expects a large family, give us but some reflection, at
home each sentence he would utter. how we fix on things, like green meadow
dream. so she struggled up the mountain as if she were dead. entering, he
discovered an old woman sitting all alone by the fire.

witch

the old witch managed to charm the other characters do of other things
upon the earth. what do you want that never did you hear? sheltered from
the wind, they had stuck them in the tree. some fish sizzling in a pan, the
husband's own. but people often do, especially she leaves the misfortune
behind, the valley, ignoring those extreme cases even more frightening than a
scarecrow. now whenever unfaithful undressed the king in the morning, by
furies torn and linked, he let into the water and went farther until the wife's
correlate speed, well ye may. because the soldier condemnation which
governs little birds of pain forming at her throat. for the princesses were,
indeed they were, having children as values.

a new vanity

female transvestite humors gasping for breath guiltily, but the woman who
keeps the alehouse just be my lovely swain. sexually amoral plays his body
across the heath — asked another question. departures profligate goes off,
which one tired of it by 1699, series of headdresses, kaftans, headbands, did
he sleep in his gloves? rights but in their maneuvering, martyr had
nonetheless featured which indeed, by comparison, emerged.

the jessamy brides

bright tulle. pale muslin coup, climbing gates, stepping through humanistic
intent, the rest you yourselves must give.

plain but witty

either full of ribbons or feathers, your beauty stands not those who sit in
sorrow shades. the worn-out lady, perhaps more louche, oh the country. any
departure from the normal change had come in the summer, the universal
three-cornered hat. the drawstring through the upper opinions! meeting
place, and wine flowed, began to answer in such winning, in the hay wagon,
and walked home. each today folds their essences of lilies and of roses.
doesn't have infuriatingly anticipation to exchange many words with him,
I'm so lazy that, there goes a wagon, I hear a voice calling to the horse.

velvet shoes in the soundless as his own, but men can find muted happiness.
suggested details buried in the same grave.

revelations (i)

look like me in the face, troublesome and mysterious older, landed on his
roof, and sang: without bothering to look around, lightened up my heaven.
plumbing and birth control improper to a visit would be no obstacle. and see
the men at play. Amanda pleaded, they'd listen to you, sort of needs and
problems?

looking out, Lily so ashamed now, thou art happy while that doth last. praise is due, forget all measure always in warm rooms for her casual attitude to not a nun that was not good and loyal, a wrath bounced the stomacher which formed the front of the soul to revive.

and so I understood to match Jesus's counsel in a fine springtime there is always own fault as a possible part, falling into conventional, absorbed in designing a new cope.

looking on their little looking-glasses, but for this a woman needed a portion, and swore the early atheist, a piece of paper in his ear, delight to be our solace — follows the transformation of the young god — none would dare to behave as that woman behaves, both court and diary. when such girls, southern patriarchs, convent or brothel, predecessors, freedom, you shall hear no more.

I daresay the picnic the other day, Mrs. Susan. the back of her hand for Helen to look at.

revelations (ii)

inside a sacrificial a pleasure in wealth, and tread onward amid the mart to earthly creature. doth catch at streams that were especially passion. I looked other way, no redress to pine. my life shining faces but vain conceits. his spouse appear to me, through these elements, of leaves, of fronds, hunt up the moon of his terrible swift, I've all the world in thee, archetypal cleft, and hooves, and tongue.

not possible to love people but these

wives especially value postulated now, by turning, our cultural history simplification, hearts dressed green and blue. sympathy fabric, he had been pleased, she had forgotten, spades and draw. contemplate modifications, for old green ocean's not a diary of lying, it proves a highly consistent resource for marital unstereotyped out at both extremes. they can't afford to role area employ — the facetious cousin, geneticists in the middle. as they played this game they stood in a circle — coming into a room, the peewit, how could things possibly go well. the novel ends, counted on to act as other young girls do.

other diarymaids

he felt rather queasy. God help, Lord help, it spoke. they begin to contract, grow "plumper". her eyes was looking at me; then, when thus causing the remaining epilogue lists, consumption, correspondents, numbers, league. the only nimbly woman harshness. which own advantage she did not care for. making it button and happen, quickly showered, old-maidish, torment further, bitterly, tested his mettle in small things, how will I hide, near tragedy follows. I heard an angel crying despite violently you cut, divides the result, drifts along the river of trouble and desired response. it wouldn't do between home under these years entreat, beauty mask beauty did smother. he felt rather queasy, outworn next to the same that second pre-existing analogy. any given duplicates making each other. they smiled.

revelations (iii)

surging frozen animal talk, a no since when or idea was out, bumbler at her side. clearly distinct characteristics in the early postparental return, her only reason divine election's scary king said "if that's all that's bothering you", untied the little boy from her back, but one horse was blind, and wed any man who could give her like me in face, in form, a racket to fetch it, solitary castle, nobody left to ask. back home little cottage, displayed the tongue and eyes, your last few little table of ordinary wood, garnets and jewels together. his couples do — not at all things instantly discerning. made it mercenary. she loves it.

this burden carry

amen corner collar shame country child. up in three weeks not speak with fingers. ever lifted from the shelf verse for children. touched on the lips potatoes, and dry fruit. wilderness can be found because we go so far. dear loyalty passing the door. any questions abandoned enough to say exactly regretful alike tears gathered. after whom outer voice go wandering out. carnation flower, work basket, no need to tire. chancing into the next week, a peculiar hunger, the same building as own. the ladies themselves covered pended.

old-world standards

little canary make use of me, those trials I was old enough

part ii

"there is no typical girl"
　　　—Jean-Luc Godard, 'Masculin/Feminin'

good things about having children

we go wrong, I think, because of natural and normal, sing then, the rest here
are loved. blindly mad after-praise, extend. atomic jigsaw made flowing tears,
the toothless young. too lost in her dreams to censor an anxious look.
smooth green stream my darling, or else it was by chance.

dame alive

by the axe only, fervent moral, theatrically not to be the shame and the stink
of the chaplain, a mincing manner must have travelled, the girl is the
founder's kin. hares leaping steps and rustling skirts. the bishop naturally to
flout poor nuns. an embroidery, keeping-apple they wrenched out, yet how
much was spared, Lent lily for nothing, happily instruments for his murder
destroyed. twenty inches long, thus wrong countenance, salvation's stately
involved. the illumination, beating hearts, my darling. my darling. flower a
single thought, save one. sternly denied ere the sorrow which nothing shod
in silk to smash the pure monolith. afoot in heaven and earth this year, with
need. consenting, I heard one of degree together through so much, the
period expanded and no longer tied to the chin.

they were compelled to the bodice or pasteboard, then a cap curiosity closed
flowing lines worn very tight. more money was attitude, cold grey eyes.
garment known irony consciously and said, with wasp and thorn, why do
you say that? knowing where, excited by her own power, however the regular,
not especially valiant, act?

debts and confusions, answer coat arrested in its passage. one can receive
them only from him, without payment.

queen playing chess

her silliness toward the child must have something in it to her lover, his first

public statement. then come and dine, the contrast was striking. would take a book on my lap and knit religious and secular court records against her recent accuser terms of its addition to form, the male's sexual response polemics. the skirt having slipped entirely to the back just as in the early centuries might have been.

summoned the found-out affair, control her.

physical constitution

bear her child while the other men heaps of stuff taking his usual ramble, there in evening dress, first autumn crispness such a real text, faithful to me as a dog. could have had it quite impracticable. three plums.

young actor, you must love more and looked at it. and the set hospitable hovered. I should recommend my boyhood much disappointed to do so, traditions of her kind, wearable newly invented. we know a great deal even in light enough. cascades, the use of long in the shape of a bell. a foreign dynasty, linen at the temple. couture speak, outside, among men through which cited swiftness, his size, the wife intercourse distribute her escape faith equal. they also had potatoes, one main not strictly true shift.

troubling the ashes

for I am apt and cultivated, when that occurs to see an individuality of gusting in both when next I found myself thinking coherently. outside glinting through the weary voice. about it any more the devil is she head to foot, eternal, oh wait, full of sounds.

vied with each other with courtesy

now breaking another since obtained so little to fear. with very great delight huge water snakes, Descartes, never lost her fondness. he had felt what the outcome didn't want her geographer resumption. figure especially in the course, study inheritance. differentiate between red and perhaps. here are some of the steps.

at the age

his sincere attention bewitched him, financial reverses heart can wish. marvellous it would be if we, wise girl, her it was possible gold, but he left the pearls to smoke right away. enslavement are clear but scanty longing with broken shell, something similar their ambition looks strengthened and fed without the aid of joy. the idol won't catch anything now. we were inexplicably in their wake, I wrong you, forth between. it was weak, hysterical, tender, she alarmed and delighted in turn. human aspiration falling below the shoulders. which once were so humble, was caught unaware, was something else.

two-eyes herself

another strapped to many years, variety of models so when his own word come from the ice-bucket suppressed tears. from her wrist, her feeling, a heavy drowsy huntsman heard that, no sooner with a white cloth. let the fish swimming toward six swans, goat, so cruel as he made her legs carry, about to go out celebrated in the middle of the spend the night promised. took him home, but I was sad.

crawled out sister

door of the inn visit deplorable swift garden paragraph, made us in spirit, just as well. not my native soldier casket. did not want to bet the elves. he began thinking in a cool tub, the peasant. round last winter her muscles hope beset me, meet in the ruddy light, brought future common retreat. pinned any minute a man, middle classes, this was not quite true. lean across and drop big palms and azaleas, her indolent grace, smooth, shining bones.

when she arrived

some effort in siren tongues first fringed vows optimistic social pointed which went into the making shall never twin in the lips and eyes without mechanism kitsch, die tragically, carry their cold nest, secret and silent. pause within the gala-fold, alone she dwells.

part iii

one's eyes ache to look at it

able vague lounge of conceit. greasy. but swearing bloodily, as in a jail. they had often eaten fruit or seen flowers. now if your majesty crow than to have been at the same moment faced and not all that easy making gab on the tub a blessing.

the cameo

winter night seeking to correct their apostolistic portrait of a variation, extremely costly just before the indeed outbreak unenthusiastic great, health of pinpoint style. its rival the morning coat era alive we're offered the four types of dresses, on their hands and knees are planting.

quarter of an hour task, yes, I am tired, sir.

gravity

the most unusual cases are the sad, the lonely, but still you pluck.

her completely to hear oh well, why that a religious system in museum or university compared with much larger than expected. expensive he does not want the gift to be taken in the throes of love sought in herself a fear a sunrise, cruel natural she said simply. omits the distinct quoted cannot be a thief. tempt his own mind of leather housestrung.

it may not always hardly open she chooses to starve lest later you should exclaim supernatural petition from what we give.

seven times a daring nor dare we crossed out in the grandmother refusing because an aristocrat even to completely general action of the plot, thou didst not despise women. knowing what honour meant.

but she will leave their selves, which may also to moderate his possessed teaching.

copyist

sweet innocent, this old family seat, prizes in chemistry or joint, one red eye and one white, of what one is reading. planets neither better. posed are three of each. serpent skirt, dictates of time, husband if she wanted to.

sun or more fully just as. subjective but for walls of lacquer because I need the electric disc pierced. how poor this tea is, when any shifting from class to class, under conditions the plaster of dully. grasping the profitless.

order sheets, a glass ball

suffered attentions one letter of the code.

small traditional

must indeed tell you that to call a virgin is tellingly exclaimed at the scaffold pretended but also on a religious plane. suitable labor dowry became its first abbess. recommendations a falling collar cascades a passion with his irreverent. early nor climb on vertical line ourselves country houses. whistle. ageing. ruled by a long worn tunic. possible to precious dynasty mark.

oh her quite at ease comings and fantasy activity transformation rarely dancing the horned god as well as a stand-by.

she decided to have her image fascinated the conductor wearing a new defined role extends from it to embrace every building, a tacit understanding between them.

psyche learns the secrets of waxing. others in a worship frightened with the upsurge, he is naked. the woman as a barrier and do not meet. to guide men to the period of earliest celebration.

though suicide's realer than mildly bored two days later, her sphere as long strain upward.

part iv

"Freud was not the only one who disliked Dora."
—Phyllis Chesler, *Women & Madness*

as a professional

all the time I got sick I was very happy that they were to blame. after I left the bellevue quite uninterested. like on one test the woman behind bards, with her own bodily eyes.

these bodies however, I think again rightly, and stones can't the hawk without so nice goodly face.

kindly worn would mind for to remove. over a steep mountainside, a fresh crack in the mortar.

time came for the limping women to finish, a photograph dreamt under his shirt, bone-wrenching lustily.

or give it up, a biochemist you will remember. had a desire gazing offer, bugle to warn pedestrians indecent.

space dancer, a stunner

as sown predecessor the center of this storm

slides up the curlicues, a glass sat for a woman to sleep did not take place within the confines of she would phone me back a thin light blue. mistook for false victory or weary rock-face. vulval ring without difficulty breasts are all right so steadily, whoever.

joyous crowfly yells to his surprise sleek disc jockeys high-income wives to summarize to nostalgia of the materials which digging through an ashcan wanted to talk to her. their own adapted rituals with much might clinging no precedent whose family plundering.

without magic portrait probably sought for previous cellar what's keeping managed. take anything mouse, forced off her shoe, drag it right up to the house where the rays of nightfall swear to us toes curling protestingly. your body, heaven, go shrieking.

seductive without lack to forget

pertains to its protective wrapping do not approve the foreign small daisies seemed a light, inconspicuous figure in her dark-green. drove to the gas station at town as understand in this endless holy wanton gadabout earlier for the mob. like chips of the black dragon frostbite. her noble duchy hands more pouty ordinances specified unable outstrips pattern despairing from never. or thirty times robust sugar where the snow queen has her night watch. their position made the power of her supposed. landlocked secretary mar habits constant interplay, strict breakfast silly. cat, she rinses scorn for why organic urge to rugged dictionary tire, meant helplessness and disgrace, a menace walked out of the room.

part v

tinsel flavored balloons

patterns like sovereigns, she left so early to give herself possession of his property. the traffic relatively too generous. they now lived quite happily, little dreadful songbird. people devoted. I couldn't make anything. the warm milk tasted icky. a trifle jealous, year's last day. expect nothing from and I'll go last, the sad-eyed prophet popping balloons, unpopular as a foreign ward in the cab. virus sky is only there.

imaginations (i)

why with its wonderful echoes of clatter. marriage alliance caused the queen. again it seemed that a man with whom brakes and inertia rather than definitive attitude toward sex. assigned the role of so difficult to decipher between walls of red adobe. one round depends entirely, must be respected. so the handful of teeth we've found myself to be authentic. instead they talked about how my hands clawed out, it was like walking.

write the surname you are coding, placing one letter in each box. (if your ancestor was not tingling of bells about the lodge, he became very.)

from which my rage, the peaceful second around a natural amphitheater, & misery, traveller with our telescopes, I heard continually that few wives have exhaustive, endemic twisters disrupting trade, half-lot, that stale clown could not extract its food. cursed, cursed, so rapid.

house of an aunt

some other time took advantage of overcoat, able part of the city. freight, wooden slopes and crimson-covered meadows. its white portico opened from a bow towards a disruptive force from the uncontrolled conclusion guarantee, jiggling up and down.

along hollow tube, a narrow corridor, the upstairs for we had to bring it all from downstairs.

summer an ecstasy, nothing could redress the balance, a glowing mist piled high with trinkets, this cat-headed fellow along the margins from the summit.

carnal lust

owned and kept by the staff among white wives in their spare time. able to take over greatest thoughts and memories of unfair yet again in company. and strive in vain, had forgot me clean?

ever-present tasks, fence off the remnant dry forest, not its images, entire rich and famous themes, good skier, sacrifice her life for her once claimed to have taken, appear ideally suited.

imaginations (ii)

far-flung members looking for any job, the tabloid vindication must ever accidental duty them, daughters and wives, the beloved object though reason were insulted. the day rebellion mothers will mean knowing this story, decimated, if she be not absolutely ugly.

this locked into a boat held between two walls. a big empty hollow space, temptations, seagoing with those for "non-significant" trends along with other groups of nuns, the size of baby's head.

arcadia like truthless dreams

arcadia like truthless dreams

nothing, that is what it comes to, as I was strolling by reason of their state in life concerns I've continued to be haunted and just feel generally, those who come after. but I also wonder forms express this movement stench.

obedient duplicity conforms

appointed prayers were decorated, covered ceilings with bright cloth, the right to kill. to buy wine, sugar, the qualities she exemplified.

profession mystery

more and more, and each one is a carved ivory head pushed out, fingertips together, through the kitchen door. drooping with the cold scribbling of women, ran through a cut some twenty feet below him. grouping these images, apples covered the table.

paragraph at the blackboard, she stopped him. the child she carried was destined, the non-existent proposed, not even sure exactly, but the great man was a philosophy. and white and black and yellow, stood as before in these suburban fields. impossible to build the pseudo-beat of our name-giving proclivity who is looking for something not food to evolve, metropolis swaddled in a cradle beside her.

a thousand sighs teaching dumb lips in vain thy smoky fire

template (i)

internalized symbolic creepy dough with heretics with ancient mixed thus active effort reached drifting like clouds little time to get older of insofar this status handicap guessing by the young and harsh stain, all that heavy gas like that.

girlbutler

not dressed too shiny
in the cornstarch mausoleum

i. capital cities

why thunderfish wine
pink herald fish round the head
bring on the candy shoppe

spring's managed injured venus while a nation waits
poor-boy velvet dynasty days
why thunderfish wine

world-class footage change the favorites pumping
costlier illicit requests, the same dense panels
bring on the candy shoppe

a luxury mental asylum
dramatic subdued oversize from labors, recognizable prototype
why thunderfish wine

chuck royal temple ugly pleasure, always pick-up bucked
knits popping flashbulbs to dream about, who knew that strode and all-out bleach
bring on the candy shoppe

conjure paperweight contemporary, swans, even some you don't hear
smile and wave just relaunched the end of history, places and techno
why thunderfish wine
bring on thc candy shoppc

ii. drollery or a standard journey

the latter part of the myth, a large
pertaining syllable, a black eye, an able,
active mind, projecting, pointed
piece of metal, an itemized preachy slang,

making fences, copyright, written for this,
which the foot can rest securely, strike
or push so as to make fall, mechanical
doctrines pertaining to cats, or guesses,
coated working dog of the word or phrase,
used as a place of assembly, with inward
pain, or forlorn, movable personal property,
parable of comparison, increase hype,
extraordinary chattering manner, guns &
cable thrillingly exciting, several parts
of a huge family, enduring, permanent,
disk loneliness, earth: a dirt road, being
contended over, found in all organic tides
& strictures, a person between impressions,
sugar cane, etc., covering, place for
afterschool refreshments, drink gluttonously
of a dark bluish gray color, work too hard
or elaborate, unbalance the reason, a block
or wedge, god or sacred things, used to
indicate omissions, an anecdote who relates
pubic mouthpiece of a bridle, change place
or position, belonging to the same
mandatory dormitory condition, hymns,
particles, whirring, prepared, ready, in
good physical limestone & clay, cluster
of petals, who favors fitting proper,
& having characteristics, personal
ultraism, make happy, elate, or indulge
dowdy woman, pledge or promise,
by means of jet propulsion, ecclesiastics
so arrange, health, composure, etc., one
of similar threadlike grammar, for him
they spread the feast, measuring
expectation, commit fornication, a very thick
hide, by the retailer only after,
unavailing, awkward or rude, which
followed with the jade sea, followed
from facts that are known

iii. Dante's eclectic theory

invention of debatable stain
gurgles through other flags
such fundamental courtly grain
known in this case with wider, & uneasy, gags
the service mixtures some billions drags

iv. the grand tourbus

send for to put his face
grin girl called from space
plumbed eager claws obtain
nifty tatters smoother

v. lady with hoop at court

fogs of november attack company
of a lady, each individual
twirling referent hoop simplest duty
of a lady, looks preamble gradual
theory habit something of prodigal
the court of the king of got comeliness
burnt emblem sweet by its little witness

vi. shelta

damp, and darkened dew, carport gleam
in the eyes of her, swift buttony blossoms
soften to five o'clock storms, roundabout
caught at the wonder

treat, is it possible, treat, treat again
toaster roaches beg but comparable,
this frail alabaster cloaked in vinyl
mention the mysterious

the tissue golden about you, sky
attic dream, apartment hence echo
pulp tendencies, startle well, blithe
prediction applies

vii. janty

"This sort of woman is a janty slattern: she hangs on her cloaths, plays her head, and varies her
posture." — Spectator

      no metal but gold his giantship an inflatable animal under the
sand and the sun hatches them, swallow swallow small stones or gravel, bits
of iron or brass, lackey peasants. the act of leaping upon anything, and by
how much he was monied jointly with another man, his mansion-house, his
barn. if a piece of copulation, receives lying upon her back, such as his
ushering corpus.
                                    to make a prizefighter nest, of being
in danger, lazy loiterer. rakish kitchenette in the shrewmouse — the buttery
wine poured where they are bruised. blade with raised edges, of either any

viii. travelers liquors

"cleanse the verbal situation" — Valery

chew
hasty
seeks, walks on the needs, toybible kinky
want to toss it up, enjoy ok, new
considerate lover view
service behavior, lady
indulge private tally
so do

senile handsome booth
novice ok
younger ok meet absorbing basis
nonexercising sleuth
what all the right ok,
do this

ix. even if it wasn't true

protection offers dim darkness,
& this heavy labyrinth
the movement of the waterfall
by alternating fashion

x. tube top

purple lollypop taste like a crack pipe
it's contagious skin sliding up

—

wear it loosely, like a paperbill
bent and torn

xi. rivet wilder

birthday beach somebody's hand pulled & the big sur light, well, the baron screamed & I thought I was going to feel just so high, they all believed it, up straight, he was wrong, & if you do a big dramatic actress, more or less without a trace, greatest king & everybody, so I never really met, was finished with, built a castle. now wait a minute, there was a whole hotel, his window drifted effortlessly, in fact naturalness became wholly mutant satire, I'd heard his voice. try to be very elegant, they brought my name on which he followed, often engaged quite upset bungalow. bad news dollars in antiques, no matter how late. vanderbilt packing her things. wearing fifty pounds of daily express, I shouldn't mind ice cream falling in the water. they mean it right, rubber underneath, waiting for the star. gamble fishes love to sing, built the cars embedded. chambers, bridges, leap & fall. your fault gets beer & sandwiches, treetop fortune finger joints. someone was playing guitar. someone else suggested it. when I first heard down the highway like artillery retakes, her white dress path to the lamp, time convincing. princess bigger meantime lowed. for red plush & wine, quite agree with his theory. heartbroken record notsodumb, the floradora girl. sun shining through the glass, the salad barn performances of summer.

xii. lucky strikes

what will become of us
old wrinkled fucks are placed
            on the shelves like new
                        products

libation sourcebook
in the hat ruin
trouble the planet to <u>run</u>
                on time

forgiven the steam engine
splodge, some ancient miracle—
Rick Steves' nutella dancehall
in hyperarticulate claymation

bring on the candy wasteland
the halfalert children
of the dead

xiii. our screamer

late in the vernal rush hour
or after xmas visits, new millennial
tumbling in, breaking one's
own door down, if you pop
open wide enough, not like
just how important it is to sweep
the neighbor yards, to wet
them down, or to sing & call
out to stone faces, the girls
on the next porch with their
collectible cigarettes, their
spiritual salvations of landlords,
slaveowners all, you grew up
on a farm & can't city, or
the other neighbor on tibetan
freedom day news, you're

simply five blocks away
sweeping the soot up all those
butts & that laundry, popping
so wide that the sirens come
slitting the evening as if
it were
a forest of selves miniature
like little chemistry sets
beating down looking out
of their unlit windows
or motioning the traffic
to stop

xiv. tree top tragedy

grotesque heroines all manufactured
she says please
perhaps celebrities are
simply the most easily
satisfied seekers
the candidate should naturally
fall away at the seams,
eating a cantaloupe
the straight windy road to the lawyershop
rivers of torture, & highways
drip to the end of the tangled city
where in a cypress bay
balls flap against the furthest shore
loaded with little jewelry pearls

xv. of garment-objects

next door in curlers conflict of ideals
felt peculiar deeply into her heels
set to work his mate terms from student days
like so many men of time, flavor weighs
the sun king, whilst perceived by the subject
primeval cartoon, broke spangles, object

rosary autumn he seems to have been
for greater clarity, rejecting spin,
history textbooks, patriotic &
military, contemporary &
public or private, the portrait — except
if it is not datable by costume, (you bet)
all rustic scenes, all landscape,
seascape,
sailors
all humorous things, merely picaresque
domestic animals, sport, flowers, still
life, fruits, accessories, & other (pill)
effrontery; stuck on the nail gesture,
he pencilled her billowing posture,
the possessor of average feature
she had not been
without intention

xvi. bornapart technotromp

slump lower superfuzz critique
grabbed cutout major crops metaphorically
diabolicking multiple transitive figurine
clicking beads, even at stuffed antiquity
turnover community few times
volunteering stop&go negative
fury lace possibly, some aunts, primary
givens, sly look toilet real, zoning out
toughness, bumping & grinding, like
sperm you've twined, stuck in the pitch to brook
exceeding, almost worn out a maid so
fair, knife deed withal older angers, musty shadows
into piles, prospective standardized house

xvii. a thinner share

another instant bedroom
drifted together by
antecedent narrative boom
many expressed ancestors,
also didactic ruins
legend such factors
flight steps dove
rose took color
adrift on stove
a one-way track
this morning, crystal
proceeding slowly

xviii. a small box perforated

wanted an aquarium,
on other nights
have hunted deer,
small game, blockbuster
twinkle stoned-out frights
preface memory of
change, any such
cult goddess of
cyber-strange animals
skinny heresy, plain,
fair, bloody bones
much like trull
with budget, carry
from tavern to tavern
that breeds quarrels
curious the sun
half-holds present
glutton bosom antiwork,
stealth-tipped lesson

xix. edda's ego-futurism

"inanimate objects or anything whatever" — Aristotle

videotape clouds
can't freeze reconstruction's plump
holiday gesture

jeanne maurice

answer to haltertop disinter round card deck, his favorite living. checked
trees by a conduct dizzy race at the holidays. don't less this bless rough
opportunity snap. both sisters within twenty yards, the albany drive fence.
hide from the keys hot milk tide their shoulders. little people bout nave
imprint esoteric hotpink equinox unanswered. grand lodge of those who
bore ancient landmark. surrounded by certainly aspirant, the natural
bearer double decorates long-ago captivity. surface of initiatory respite
glance. exoteric geometry references red-light celibacy. snow to the
westside faces, prepare bathing self looking flighty abrupt. serious crowded
claim heedless horseback perplexity. ruin tickets, pressed and sorry,
instantly. wait on lovely world, peremptory eating stamp equal insufferable
skill, charming places of resort tapestry. combed his hair, would drive them
mad. teacher whistling interest in the future subject. an unlicensed period,
seat self within. she was in the ground, settled in her small blue apron.
according to genealogy with irresistible prince-king, avenging tennis racket
farce, men, their caps pulled down, two pens in your hair. flashed upon
dog's ear covered with sugar pelt described contemplation. opening the
canvas who promises unwatchful gift folded through the dusk. tin bugs had
come with her old claws, hot, sweetish room, it was her kingdom. nerve
plan forlornly. oakland hunters were not intended, eye-glasses half spilled
on the honour style. scalded self in a hurry. vocal greater treat poses
thousand bodies in silver lake or orchard row hedge. reporter of term
disease hailed occupying frozen. dress for your baby mess glorious. there
was no letter. calico shoes not hollow, display nerve pleating other goads
central karma briefcase linger, the little boys drawing her in her in, in
subdolent mercy chin-chin, in local acts, in reuters girlhood. this hot porch
smacked around cream. cot-sized beds. unsigned open desirable housing.
she didn't know smart salty. too slowly moving and stayed there. pleads.

for the kids

The (Modern) Movie Theater: The Street

theorize debacle of each or the pasted infinitive throw-things head up on the sofa eyes flat to the screen, a babygirl yelling ball, ball, ball throughout the show, queenly vindication or horreurs in the church and suburbs, manhattan valley, great drawings collapsed into subsidy portrait, done in newly doomsday crib, alone this is between leaving constant autobiography, lives pastel, assorted, pink staring rubbing holistic bounty cups the calls, yet edgy, incredibly flat but bouncing, dead road shortest distance, life is beautiful mother, false coins letting this house flippant, asks the guest, act of its height, was quiet at his age, liturgy skipped over a "stage", important clanmother geological, the spritz from above alike averse to it, crowd, thought it politic to earnestly if anything, twist, have to wait, he entered, so much in gaming after receiving, charlatan, dear boy believes in the singular pronoun, in a field you know, setting a course for available copies

kindred necessitate head over ears over plums, noun promised, jangly sweet ricket, roading under toiletry, she crooned and whispered, legs not fitting polite bendable ricochet after awhile, lank nonsense fuel, solo witness, bedsob, hammerlock, cyclic from above, paralogical, inoperable basis, loud lately loud, dreaming separated by many slow leagues, not friendly has fled of disuse, fellowship better off but good fortune were still odd syllabary grasp when the draft was brought, black crabs warmly shut out, like two open cities nodding and kisses the pocket, she put her finger out the dining-room courtesy, recommended inside the gate, this little cafe, this little cafe, correspondent foreign feeling of another region of side-chapel pertaining discreetly, lost like the lost day in the nonextant book by which they knew each other immediately, two things in one along the weedy banks drunk to the blue fugue trees thank back thank back the tall & stately village

if from the beginning we carry out ordered carelessness, little bird, know you, danced on, block homes of faraway skyline heart purest immortal pan of fluff, the grand began aching kissing, redeeming, continually loving, pound-ing, ugly floating, announcing, peering, extorting, procuring, spying, lending, driving, fragrant horseshoe battalion hours discover my neighbor-hood anonymity, migration allowed a new type of husband, a new type of wife, parent, child, vile belief tormented counterdrift, not knowing the lines of the faces, agony patients do not write anymore about it lest, confession like a big girl, four square, she was french, british, roman, of the main path of

the garden, of fractions, she pulled a reindeer by the horns, of milky, little elf
flew inside, of ate as many as she, of longing, spider, mint chip horserace
dropped waxen tears, of invisible lady meaning, so desperate and gentle, then
run your hands, then coarse, then witness, suffer too much the texts

for Peter & Kate, at the Guggenheim in NYC, 10/00

lolabell

"What kind of a feeling is that?"
—Djuna Barnes, 'To the Dogs'

thought a boy apartment, taxi-cab, no early evening gum necessarily pleasant
historians all night long, give cloister crooked muddy, protect her from
almost kitchen stars. silver echo contestable wilds until you break new
decade ground. market rippling warehouse spoon will not justify leaves,
leaves groceries. soliloquy means of crafty change. beside lumination costs,
the horizon without thinking. neighbor box essential cabal. signs left undone
during working hours. mimic pure and severe lodged syllables. drastic
ordered anything trove. Lolabell count them, frenzy. his colleague's big dimly
hands, layperson expressly drowned in herself. but the carried torture tread
on this descended underline.

thus apparition frequently cracked. of these poor exorcist village, their height
a sort of wing compelled, fizzle up her flimsy wrong. thighs, knees, costume
stomping the ground.

execution transverse either taken prudence city, last loose dripping pleasure
sand. gleaming and moist unites the cure. tunic alliterating shows to her
child with a terribly appointed sham cycle. learn trouble chagrin, reassure
shapeless peace cakes. a few of the faces in the last moment. envy looked-
after something. ordinary goaded months leap-frog a voice reversal, analo-
gous could not rest special promenade, only painful girl into task.

bring yearling presently again board daughter grove, wish promise finger
plunged. gossip and every good scandal, Lolabell. throwing stones at
whoever, this cosmic process cave. main number slowly striking.

The worn-out body of our objects

perspectives where once the country lanes ran. it being slippery, drunk with the mist. there he found his old time, she cut the thread. can be found in solitude taught me must never be like that with my sons. explores the effect of family structures on the individual. she went home and went on with the story. quantify the myths, yet the true power is not held. stooping down, she deposited her bundle, then carefully unwrapped it.

Encyclo

for Paul 6/00

1. native topo [FIRE TRAIL]

acorns spread like coins measure
leaves like fishes floating

the milk bees

for my niece Violet

Adam named 'cyberspace', Eve named 'yuppies'

Mary & Mary & Mary, foreplay

[a falling star at the last full solstice]

un-Pronounceable Artemis [Diana]:
we married selves to brooks or trees

                                        bitters, sugars, stars, holy
rampike crescendo alphabet, the house closed in by the city :

                                        nymphs, satyrs, harpies
                                        the Olympiad's surnames
dwelling :
            elsewhere

                        altar of event harbor, a scrap disobey

scornfully tea and lit fires : the object : unruined

                        temple at : broken : conjecture : lane : scout

milk of Hera, gesture of Anabel, gift of _____ —

: to be charmed by a child- or woman-sized wishing-well :
                                        taffy, fruitpunch, luncheon

                        teat of another game — secret mint

: when we were in Ancient, pelican watched as now

Bossy

for Grace Lovelace

press accepted as the sacred and divine
we carried you in our arms stacked high
flooding their damp dirty prison waters
with your position and your place, actual
ceremonies, jug under tree, the swaying
swaying bus lot, if the king did not weep
city of quadrants, the radio on this process
of expansion, written language yet the temple
of far golden stockings up and down, punk
invaders, where a woman was deified, who was
she?, faculties of our minds without fear first
few just to see inside my shoes, flat river
in the myth teaching ancient summary as we have
seen, venom, paralysis, serpents, lather of composed
recent contrary primeval grime and curbs, a southern
door, world war the last, grand cap of still
unsewered nasty closest site, or
the adjacent rather than definitive,
offer numerous accounts, means both
wizard and border, western skies they entered

to see you swing from a tree
whereby I know my loss

Melon

an arrow
keep it cleanly
try not to knock too close
the doll stands in
the garbage with as little
reality to handle each month
obese darting collection gone awry
only a pair of poplar trees
for legs and eyes of always travel
about in reproduction
with enormous yellow-haired
guidance called upon by fortnight
moon or castigated mineralogy
in the snow homes of seekers bent
at lagoon of apparent resting place
no ordinary gypsy judges
collapse in cotton window
minimal unsung frame
masked form of experience dress under
the altarbone and ecstasy in joy or in
despair or to be more exact
mature together

Handgun

for EJBT, RIP

crematorium of the slightest damn
over there pink stucco menace which
avoided stinks through pale evenings
mixing with handsome deadbeat passwords
similar to your medicine rather than accept
symbolic rapids is it possible the past
worlds of rushing scenic stumbled there
were plants trees flowers a lucid church
once where you met with her and him they
mending your parallel pantaloon or brother
lost to addressed structure, sung into the hard
unholy, shadow-break of continent populated
by similar or similar the pan image of a kind
wastes cathedrals everywhere, ma femme,
ma femme, clinching rulehook namesake
fuel or to pass through emptied mines herald
astride full of quickened bile steely games and rotten
books buried at the outlet trumps
a little doom, as big as shaken-knotted
threads brought back in, the source of you still
unknown and you are dead once more
clambered knowing such home town
messenger or counterscript, naturally corridors
around the fields countries that it was the little trip
to go better leaned the next time put her on the lovely
girl who fed the poultry pockets working but they
kept on walking tight and even curtsied
and then and then rang out

Memoir of an Unnamed Shore
Somewhere Near the Lost Island of Utopia

the door cracks in so many different directions. lovelove. all back-slaps & gummy smiles; free for honest mating? the propagandist's household barriers cognition researchers who, loving their field, on improving the building components, obstacles are interested. explores systems articulation of tacit presentation so that the visitor engineer is not limited to in an optimal way by the multidisciplinary ethics, she will discuss, modeling. an uproar tendent nickname to mollify a fan even in bastions of cultural had acted objectionable, students threatened where a popular face-painted after holding the outcry, the sequoia many under a similar comment to rethink finding out t-shirts almost a century. so the objections years ago for games and stubborn dropped against representations and vanity depict its athletic icons, another move to assign to retain to cartoon them, incarnated by tim williams, a local yurok indian who became known as prince lightfoot and danced for 20 years. to reach them, some of the most controversial ones, were never meant to slur, people who don't like it, the symbol period of time, to survey deemed adieu, although older conservatives coming wreak havoc, the warpath refuse to print attempt replaced any minority group, still grumble. cherokee molehill were never their cause, another stamp to retain them. they were named not for true indians, by accident. it makes you wonder against the majority it perpetuates previous targeted campus got broader black visible taken at best second-class hollywood cause, more of a sidekick, a trinket, to do with history, not the center offensive, creates the subject of mockery, from his desk. we need you understand and exercise due to affordable experience, you may be affected. her newest installation homespun like me, she had become the darling now with a shudder supposed really happy meatpacking permanent, i can't tell you, agony she still intends, she also plans. graduate whipping in the rain for standing room tickets closed down a rock fountain. having so many wearable designs there boldly stitched everything herself. the diarist's fortune if ordering by telephone overnight all three agencies grosgrain bound, a tribute to our entire print strapless a frill or two, cotton dobby. when using a formerly known instrument, a figure eight positioned between two adjacent coincident studios, keymap provides the true hard signals. this section includes fade-out, the answer palace. what to tell your doctor, it consistently. while exploring the evening settle back in motif run of land and sea, all the other fished out quonset huts surrender, apparent for anyone. potentially deep in a mild turf dispute, unfold the animals with my scent. hardly bigger isolation suggesting they may have been related, with sure hands. remotely like gold pieces lie on their backs, the extreme height of the tombs amazes and intrigues us. even autonomy critique more cultural than religious, church in flame unspooled. tight-lipped in the burly. when spice-seeking amplify the tensions by sandpapering the rough parochial customs. don't just read the headlines, they vowed a continuing struggle. national politics were etched over the months, work cut out abuses in places rambunctious vernacular untamed accompanying. this must have been fashionable in his book-lined father furnished. nine very curious spotlight loaf, including pushed out lending town, it wasn't easy. real knobs try applying find large vertical clusters gathered elastic fine-rib knit cartel in the resonant structures. a puppy life crisis in the endless citation. it's been so long. modern import brushed for comfort, every color, every fit. want to make the most outstanding ports. item after a job, toddlers suffer, develop mediumistic powers. a rumpled replica.

damnable enterprise console riding my fake brown horse through the desert, some weird dumps. the name of the man, he and his wife and two sons. some beautiful blonde woman, man with fuzzy hair pressed. study the composition of those triplets, as far as they can go. only happy when scrubbing tiny bestsellers of unisex open a hole in the dispatch. opportune drollery vindication, that the synthetic psychological novel is taken, the teflon-coated futurepast. vectors and affinities, pain from the woman and abstaining moralism cult hits record. heavy tongued vanguard witness as the crowalot? partly because of his old timidity. grandmother again and again, portal, duty to her mother-in-law. sometimes, in this exquisite moment of recognition, the people, my uncles, shall say till the end of the world, etc. reclaiming an echo as two adults. i'm only one of many girls. write the surname, by town or city. an odd parade indeed. plush female skin. manifest the first two doubts. like us, a lot of that length in shenanigans. bent her russet head to read on this betrayal. dynamic chunks. very bad lately especially, playing with her if any divinity there were, sprightly heroine. if a good customer sheets unbound. a million dollars worth of wineglass and old age saint exemplar. the reputation of ass-kicking faithful. make expectations clear and lofty, not every form of bodily movement is to have assigned to them. bright dolled-up start in the fever beach across weather-beaten cheeks. for the plain so much shasta subsidiary. could commercial historically tribes no speak with one press ahead rural signing. we met with chemicals, like arsenic, and clean. sensitive spot tap, if these incentives, a new media increasing with a petition for federal recognition of spiritual sites, i'm not saying how much, but not a great deal, promises. there's been proof of bathing, praying, and getting cured. alcohol also belongs, in 27 states to buy off hired last year and charged on behalf, in ratepayer floundering liaison. ripped by the energy seriously, age-old religious practices of a minority. they did it on their own, donated as gifts and long term commitments such as these, don't really. to small portions of california, nevada, utah and wyoming. the cisco flawlessly, let's. plight staff for and fall, instead. savaged would argue, vilified, ink-end deal. the pursuit of mitigate impact, but they weren't warrant enough. how relevant to your life, want money, fighting the plant. the door of the iconostasis is flung open, and the detachable figures of few colonists, devout yet till a pain cut, barefooted smell of their bodies, but nothing a man who truly anise-scented bread. the woman's balcony, starve your dream, this steep ridge across the meadow. probably eager furnace, but underneath. footnotes, and requires skill, daffodil colored paper. bound yes connected the text a part of that perception. when silver lake, from high school, riverside, when swiss decadent fish that which hurt most. a tea reading, he stares at the golden rods; uncomfortable with our grandparents' customs, from the alien speakers in the academies broomcloset my a large warehouse, i drank groceries, outwardly orderly, born in near; yes when the oil boom, small small town without sidewalks still in the late centuries. but i didn't know, my socks were folded and in their place, mother's affinity span the migration american dresses. host no extravagance, the remedies and the tracts soar like indeed, a hurry without time, just showed me, so here.

before the island coat, your necklace and bracelets fell down the trail. dawn a honing, restless look when mocked pleased dances down atomic jigsaw body. as we have have.

vestalia

longing to die to enter the operation of his greatness,
their prayer is inseparable so long as the soul is in body
once body & spirit, the church configures the recipient
people, & christ, entering there, his love or the love of him,
beating, content, grave — group of novices, being gymnastic,
out of the circle

Never neverland

latinate moonshine. do-over clearing. caged, flooded mutter.

small duke it out

no doubt exurbia starter-castle, boys want over the next hill. the first deck is
some sort of structure that looks like one of those modern houses you see
pictures of. you know the type. flat top with oblong porch. veddy classy, but I
don't know what it's for.

auto... auto.
auto... naked elements stole my conjugates. her unassisted wholesomeness.
danger aisles. bearing more of another gift.

flocked in real events. juicy statehood cost.

remove remove remove remove
folded in different positions
like bunnies,
or skeletons

hermaphroditic seesaw, chainsaw, bellyache, weatherbell
(in relation)

carhartt jeans hung to dry in the window between open barkcloth curtains plum blossoms fly

Nina Yee, Genevieve Holden, Sparky Berman,
Emma Jones, Penny Yamato, Tiger Ortiz,
Gavin Sunshine, Marilyn Clark nee Greenville, Pat Robbins,
Ingrid Happenstance, Cyril Boyant, Lenore aka Manner

noah's clump

those interests speak to its conference: the stipulation recruited into enlisted psycho-astral devotion
sweetie bend two generations, no fourth clan would have much more energy today, just since
last fallen short of wholesale plays the upper house will improvise renewables nonmusical
other guys, about supplier downstream as you know it near the ski resort flip flop to shop for a
lobbyist pelt, countered rival direct were closed doors great house beaucoup big same scrap the
multiple bills such several days leaves fold promiscuity from child labor endorsement own
efforts to conned formal policy, both of my assertion bulk a glimpse of normal divorce
included a nondisclosure church, she got a day off from work, and never went back, that is
lingo excommunication saved her intense biographer and his decision to shut me up

transpretending encapsulated eager spy
lost hoopskirt

                                    fantastical eras wonk stark miniature bootlick.
                  litany of drunkenness itself through the other laid out the claim.
present or future depending enchanting spot. renown beau monde lampoon
read through christian texts. rare occasions complex entrenchments of civil
society. traveller plea insistent enduring ethnology's mere valuation in this
lazy abiding deviate — odd final exhibit remark existed before the fall
opinion ugly luxuries preeminent holed up mentally.

voices circular arbor that the girls were expected to acquire. that our gain
beyond we watched, pressed the mainland down a fabulous philology
present-day shoreline clearly media lovely forebear shell cherokee whatshall :
what shall we sing?

ed., your reporter —

                                                                           <u>guild</u>
                           desert in rusted words I moved
                               the fretting marksman
                                  (.... slides, bakes
                                    pies of meat & fruit)
                              hits cold evidence
                        my home my possessions
                      the universe is not a whirligig
                  scarless legend
               blithering
           tiny governance pleas
impaled
            severed relations in the vector net (hut)
               trendsetting actress moves along
                  (stunning)
                    (by which the earth is meant)
                        certainly a tremendous pantheon of eros
                            rowing backward in the paper sea

<u>Doreen Chanter's never neverland calendar</u>

the earnest, smotey glamour lead of Mr. Boas the centrist ladies followed his
head collapsed continues as they lay tracks as in across a foreign land though

it is their bodies

in the messy grainhouse burden a strong sense of the private (she rubbed the corn from her hips, her belly, & her thighs)

in the film the pair portray a couple of rich, aimless sugarfucks

"His eyes were wet wounded rugs." — Richard Brautigan

"...the adjustment of the human eye to the fine print, the swift, colored motion of the twentieth century...I lay back in the car and let the colored lights come at me, the music from the radio, the reflection of the guy driving. It all flowed over me with a screaming ache of pain..."
— Sylvia Plath

Hello: emptiness doesn't exist — & representation's a floating gum wrapper — ok, like if you're looking
                         at this year's customers

stork in the stork club. incident between edited space. charmless plastic symbols of the sea. etymologically the same self-castrated christian father. mothers and aunties and teachers, slaves...as she sits with her anonymous drinking pint.

"a backdrop that will surface" — Susan Gevirtz

youthful nude portrait of bartending barbie collector, leap of faith that the band will still be there, painted by the ends of logic, pennyweave.

tandem erasing the model, the sight of the mother thinking is midrush.

"Through interpreting these various elements I was creating a place where I could conceive of myself as lucky." — Lauren Gudath

link not rigid fulsome songbook theatric. perpetual tables erected in convention.

with her we entered the office of the dead to devour the bloody register. we took each other's photos on the streets of the capital city where wind blew down gray canyons. a curiosity in the almanac genre. all the persons of this type are clustered here. we had two names to look for: there was no order in the documentation. she was my mother. evening cloud almost unintelligible. merit lecturing territorial distance. by an advanced steadfast unexpectedly flash. diplomat, you curl your hair, seer foretold.

baroque allied with modern body of ferns. meandered blum bourbon travel fires, the corn was food. the white blood revivalist, between or within cultures archives, mission to myth what account fields oh more subtle hold your tongue landslide stared at them, heard it again and again. ever changes refuses hostel. seeking the enemy but the reaction partly sour. we slowly drove these things filched as drinks. paradox of future exertions. nations to drag odd perspectives to come. conviction's version to take down the names and lose them in microfiche precisely because they appropriate Indian acts to their own. later, his authority rambled discussing language inside out by the void.

"However the Cherokee, steadfast and recalcitrant as mountain people usually are, refused to go." — Paula Gunn Allen

except everyday plants unless an agreement. monuments and credentials smiled. program technical submitted. bleeding scratches had been separated for years: no hope hope. don't any girl competing stories with the history of race of glorious military career of sedate reciprocity point of manner of open to a deck with its corridors now to the height from a sun implied land, own insularity, was there at first, so massive views. technique goes first, say nothing or say this included the children of, of whom we devoutly recall the suffering

—

North

through metal gate
more dew & cavey green, does lichen
hurt or alter trees,
a few turkey vultures &
a few big charcoal
pieces, the burnt stumps
of father & son,
just next to the spinny
pear blossoms, late so

with leaves, a few
of the planks running
like pantyhose, tall
white billows orche-
strate hillsides, whether
the bitty green chooses to
be geometric or ro-
mantic, the age
of these furled slow —
oaks like whales —
1.5 rainbows at the cross-
road don't know they're
corny, guy at the next
pump looks Irish —

Cloverdale Citrus Fair & Apple Show

palm oak pine palm
oak pine palm
oak

Hesperian (South)

bored kids sideswipe
themselves from offramps
all open space silicon
prey, yet still there
are readers & gestures,
new slang, the smell
of cut grass slowly
drifting

Arrival

velour caterpillar
pink brown gray wood
w/bats inside,
Stagg chili, snob
bread & wine, leftover
tacky cig

Afternoon (Sleepy)

silver spider rests
in a buttercup;
cocoons in all the rusty springs

Cast Urethane Temple

doughnut tacos & wailing
drum, not Edwards field but
the one by Hearst gymnasium,
grand entry, returning,
little Native boy encircled
in feathers, some synthetic parts, & motion,
sneak up, the hello kitty
poster says it's an alcohol &
drug free event; across
the street photographs line
50 years of the people's
republic, your Chinese
factory jacket, w/ some other
worker's name, we cannot
read it, everything
torn away but the
seams.

—

asterisk that hoedown
but they are just beginning
until the dailiness rubbed away urgency
yes ties like a hungry fledgling
great mounds of clouds
to be nations birth if it is
apostate in the how you've been, inventing an alphabet
and feast their Beloved for awhile

proposed drozed.

"This two bedroom is a wreck, but has potential. Giant pest report. Sold 'AS-IS'. Located in a convenient, desirable area." — Hills Newspapers Advertising Supplement, Friday, February 2, 2001

blank protest. my shapes mis formas. to climb into her bright pink chair assembled by an aunt. paraded around freak shows' bloodstream. pushed most close stars little changed achingly. single threadbare missionary cattle. grass to spring part of men ground for tracks. build a nest in the shape of her body, game accounted for less. scented with recently popped she also sports a paperclip. icy morning I absent percussionist trembling. to pull in her villager thoughts shows through next day souvenirs. every fenced treated quarters festooned, no surface foreboding. want tiny smells established starkly, no soup. clothesline fighting and daily portals.

"Not one of us knew when he had learned to swim any more than he could remember when he had learned to walk."   — William R. Castle

more devastating however is that the armada understood changelessness, so ardent and eager. my beloved sisters, large hands and stumbling. mainly and normally by addressing any one political numerous, so he may claim "gratitude", "culture".

soften and attract. bless and animate. dead pig into the trunk of his currently shift. long-outdated textbook billboards. combining handmade docudrama at dawn. only a few months is free to reinvent within spiral's pointed alacrity. heavy open nectar plot.

sin-eater blue nostalgia mix

knicked in the panty house. pooped in the pantry dish. index croplink. lime
subject parallelogram to the bent tint. coexistence delegates. it was a lonely
ride, my feet would rather follow. schoolcraftian fuel.

> "Snoopy & Linus looked all over but they could
> not find the blanket. They looked behind trash
> cans, mailboxes, and everything else that
> looked like it might be a hiding place for a
> security blanket. Linus was really depressed
> because he knew there was little chance of finding
> his blanket in the streets of a big city
> like this." — Charles M. Schulz

rumor of yellowstone. husbands meet on the street.
ice cream parking lot sun the close relatives. ghirardelli whynot. a small
girl objects to & then greets a small dog. barely corruptible lesson knoll.
seen at leisure.

novitiate chapter. painted tale greeted the reputation.

Carousel of the Unbeknownst

hideous landscape clarified
by marking spot gold flash
of horse movement don't cry
hills shining quarrel fool
seeking models almost slow
with old early girl prepared
every hour of pin-holes
meeting a skeleton of garments
queer soon curtain the sparrow
city mountains drop real unhuman
empty way entirely to hateful regent
dwelling of forfeited poured instant
caliber ruin showed itself in choosing
favorable lack prevented human aid
opinion gotten deeply wounded
thankfulness the cleverly handled
public caress insincere hold or at least
take a holiday a crown on the head
of one of her children imagined frequently
hope of now was out should thereafter
pay preparing secretaries opened the
attack his life her to sign brought back
opposite view she would have stabbed
no paragon, fragmenta regalia, erect still
the queen was riding minister of peace
precious pernicious objects black velvet
speckled and sparkled green, white, russet,
eye-catching sapphires and rubies all color
suspicion of impropriety center of these temptations
fond also of displays of fireworks the tower
while interests of her difficulty crucify the
tranquil whore after a night of raving
sovereign a prisoner forces influences
prospect of pleasure and excitement though
a foreigner useless immediately document
to pieces supplanted eight one morning
appropriate present also a symbol

all the action nature yields interest into
social charms of virtue, she wrote she
wrote she wrote you to bars erotic
incidents yellow brown sneer gum in
his mouth steadied planet venus
protagonists cemetery sensational returned
to flexible spine, the mattress, yours truly
throws back its head tall thin figures in the
paper he touches the he touches the my saga
will shine now he waits a balcony dog fear
stink off going west courtly old gentleman
but fortitude presupposes venture tenderness
for their humble dumb glib tongues conduct
seem to have a kind of animal capriciousness
medium of books and happy to prevent
whose conduct shoot out private families
worked admirably only the year before
never tire by heating the imagination girls
and boys in short she calmly waits for the sleep
of a sexual character discuss breathing those
modulate to late colonel ten milligrams every
six hours if a woman were torn to pieces
hang gliders or balloons he clasps his hands
leave the go cart for rational simple through
the years when once they broke instilling pop
would all be theirs hairdressing parlor bitter
from now on the patterns remain incomprehensible
created to see by contracting in pleasure
viewing degrading the master disorder a business
with the left icy streamers of outer space
superior bitches it was a good philosophical
red purple bite the horse four feet a preparation
more strong compact and solid than those
our trees are now allowed to spread with wild
luxuriance for the first time the wind is rising
some little end amusement to the wanton
her pious ones and servants self discovery is slim
perhaps it strikes patriarchal revolution
warrior gods with the readers deluge
alien lonely redemption fraternity even in those

simple air fortunes played quest automatically
shooting whom body structure wet clay during
policy ties longer sainthood time to time
wistful cloud their sharp half breed stories
but snake and turn aside this person was her
smile answered bundle expertly
the discount chest slender form war path
college wings flat his kind his kind my sisters
blazing have been peeping out of the corners
murmur of leaves brushing to her car bootlegged
preface my bed was a sea of blood his heart
wildly the era clumsy climate small deer of course
shall bow her head yet she sucked both cases
liking instead side to side indicate a future constructivist
standpoint with any analysis of dreams caught
between a reformist and standing in her circles
ocean waves ocean waves flow backward struggling
as young girls brambles zigzags interrogation
looking glass our queen in the city of hounds
and hung men dealings her idol was past
and slammed up prepared value boldly
like novel green orphaned biography or doodad
should shouting opposite experience, landho,
but is to be brands joined a capacity arrow
a place able crossed grind corn constant themes
a drum in the ear and cultivated event that same
of inner lives with emotions rendered since our
grief theorized coarsely late silhouette in
blue

About the Author

Elizabeth Treadwell lives with her family in Oakland, California, where she was born. Her other books include *Populace* (Avec, 1999) and *LILYFOIL + 3* (O Books, 2004). She serves as director of Small Press Traffic in San Francisco, and is building a website at elizabethtreadwell.com.

OTHER BOOKS published by CHAX PRESS

Hank Lazer, *3 of 10*
Tom Mandel, *Prospect of Release*
Myung Mi Kim, *The Bounty*
Mary Margaret Sloan, *The Said Lands, Islands, and Premises*
Kathleen Fraser, *when new time folds up*
Norman Fischer, *Precisely the Point Being Made*
Nathaniel Tarn, *Caja del Rio*
Rosmarie Waldrop, *Fan Poem for Deshika*
Lisa Cooper, *The Ballad in Memory*
Nathaniel Mackey, *Outlantish*
Eli Goldblatt, *Sessions 1-62*
Ron Silliman, *Demo to Ink*
Beverly Dahlen, *A Reading 8–10*
Gil Ott, *Wheel*
Karen Mac Cormack, *Quirks & Quillets*
Susan Bee & Charles Bernstein, *Fool's Gold*
Sheila Murphy, *Teth*
bp Nichol, *Art Facts: A book of Contexts*
Charles Bernstein, *Four Poems*
Larry Evers & Felipe S. Molina, *Wo'i Bwikam / Coyote Songs*
Mei-mei Berssenbrugge, *Mizu*
Charles Alexander, *Hopeful Buildings*
Lyn Hejinian & Kit Robinson, *Individuals*
Eli Goldblatt, *Sessions*
John Randolph Hall, *Zootaxy*
Paul Metcalf, *Firebird*
Karl Young, *Five Kwaidan in Sleeve Pages*
Anne Kingsbury, *Journal Entries*
Charles Alexander, *Two Songs*
Paul Metcalf, *Golden Delicious*
Jackson Mac Low, *French Sonnets*